# The Midlife Career Change Playbook

*A 12-Month Strategy to Replace Your
Income and Live the Life of Your
Dreams Without Risking Everything
You Worked For*

# Table of Contents

inconvenience caused as a result of reliance on information as published on, or linked to, this book.

The author of this book has taken careful measures to share vital information about the subject. May its readers acquire the right knowledge, wisdom, inspiration, and succeed.

# Introduction

Congratulations on downloading this book and thank you for doing so. If you are sick of your 9-5 office job and the daily grind, or if you are simply feeling unfulfilled and trapped in your current situation, then this book is for you. One thing that you should know is that you are not alone. The world is full of people who are unhappy and unsatisfied with their jobs. Needless to say, this has a bad impact on the quality of life. The good news is that there is a way out of this. You can make a difference as long as you put your heart into it. You have the power to make positive changes in your life.

Of course, this does not come without challenges. Although this may not be a problem if you are single, things are much different when you have certain responsibilities. For example, you may have a family to support and/or a mortgage to cover. Many things can happen in life. Now, some people shy away from doing what they want because of their responsibilities. They simply want to take the safest way, and that is to leave things as they are and stay unhappy every day. If you come to think about it, this does not solve anything. This book is not about taking the safest route in life. Rather, it encourages and teaches you to live the life that you want without being irresponsible. If you want to create positive and meaningful changes in your life, then you should work hard for it. If you want to have a career change without losing everything that you have already built so far, then this book will be your number one guide.

There are plenty of books about this subject in the market, thanks again for choosing this one! Every effort was made to ensure it is full of useful information. Please enjoy!

DOWNLOAD YOUR FREE BONUS:

**<u>Pursue Your Passion E-book</u>:**

Go to: bit.ly/PursueYourPassionNow

# Step 1 — Build up 6 Months of Savings

What you intend to do demands more than careful planning. More importantly, it requires that you take actual steps and positive actions to achieve your goal. The first step is for you to start to build up 6 months' worth of savings. Actually, this is the first step towards a bigger goal. As the saying goes, "A journey of a thousand miles starts with a single step." This is that single step. Your objective is to be able to earn 6 months of savings. This is to ensure that you have enough money to support your family, as well as to cover for all your other expenses and obligations. Do not worry; you will most likely not spend all those savings. After all, you will also be making money along the way. However, this is important just to give you a good margin just in case the worst case happens where you fail and not earn any money. The amount of money that you need will depend on your needs. If you have a family to support, you will need more money, especially if you have several kids. You should always consider your situation. Be honest with your current financial standing. If you have debts and other obligations, then you should think of those things as well. This is an important part as it will give you a sense of direction, as well as the right action plan that you'll be taking. After all, the things that you have to do will also be influenced by your current financial situation.

There is no easier and quicker way to "earn" money than by saving money. By cutting down on your expenses, you can significantly increase the money that you have. Not knowing how to control your expenses, regardless if you're a high-income earner, you'll most likely end up in financial difficulty. Let us now look at some money-saving techniques and tips that you can do

## The importance of living below your means

Whether you intend to quit your job or not, it is always important to learn to live below your means. Unfortunately, many people live above or beyond what they are capable of, and so they end up with lots of debts and all other bills and obligations that they could not resolve. Needless to say, you should never let this happen to you. If you want to have a successful, fulfilling, and happy life, then you should learn to live below your means. Now, do not think of this as something negative or that you would have to live poorly. This simply means that you need to ensure that your expenses are proportionate to your earnings. Anything that exceeds your income would mean that you will have some form of liability one way or another. Being able to live below your means is one of the best ways to save money.

It is also worth noting that you should strive to live *below* your means. This means that you need to have some excess after you have deducted your expenses. You have to be able to save money at least every month after paying for all your financial obligations. If you do not have savings, then that is something that has to be addressed quickly. It is advised that you get a pen and paper and list down your sources of income and expenses. Be specific as possible, especially when it comes to noting down your expenses. Once you have everything written down on paper, you should examine your list of expenses and think of ways on how you can minimize them. Is there something that you could drop from the list? Also, try to find out if there are more affordable alternatives for some of the items on your list. The key is to try to lower your expenses as much as possible. Take note that this does not mean that you have to live a poor and sad life. You can still buy whatever you want and enjoy life. But, you need to make it a priority to have some savings. Do not forget that this is your objective to earn enough savings that will support you for 6 months. This is not a simple task to accomplish especially if you have not yet saved any money or if your current earning is just exactly enough to pay for all of your needs.

The next step is to focus on your sources of income. Can you think of a way to increase your monthly income? With more income, you can also enjoy more savings. Do not worry; we will discuss notable ways to increase your income later in the book. Indeed, it is not unusual to find people who need to supplement their income just to earn enough money.

A common mistake is to increase one's expenses as the income increases. This is wrong. In fact, you should always try to cut down your expenses all the time. Focus on increasing your income and your savings. Once you are able to do this and you are able to generate enough money that can cover you for 6 months, then you can easily make decisions and take risks.

Next, you should compare your earnings versus your expenses. This involves just a bit of math. Simply subtract your total monthly expenses from your total monthly income. You should end up with a positive profit. If you get a negative number, then it means that your expenses are higher than your earnings – an easy and sure way to be in debt and financial distress. Hence, if you ever encountered this situation, you should do everything that you can to lower your expenses. Of course, you should also try to increase your income if you can. Still, the easiest and quickest way would simply be too cut down your expenses. If you really think about it, a person does not really need much to live a decent life. But, of course, things can be challenging when you have a family to support and a house to maintain, among others. If you know that your income is not enough, then talk to your family and decide on ways to lower the expenses. Do not be stressed out. I assure you, there are many people out there who are in far worse financial situation than you are, and yet they are able to survive and face life's challenges. It is all a matter of how well you handle these problems.

Again, if you want to save more money, then the best and easiest way to deal with it is by lowering your expenses. If you check your grocery list, you will definitely find some things that you have been buying but do not really need. There are also things that you do and spend money on that are not really essential. It is recommended that you write everything down on paper so that you could examine the situation from a clearer perspective. Again, the key is to lower your expenses to save more money. No matter what you do, you will not be able to give yourself a chance to live the life that you have always wanted unless you get to live lower than your means. Hence, this first step is a very important one that you should not take it for granted.

## Money saving tips and techniques

Saving money is not hard or complicated at all. However, take note that you do need to make some sacrifices. The truth is that you do not need a lot just to survive. There are some people out there who have proven this by living off of a mere backpack. Of course, you do not need to take extreme measures just to save money, but the point here is that you do not have to spend so much unless you can really afford it.

Saving money only requires some adjustments. For example, instead of driving to and from work that is only a few kilometers away from your house all the time, you can just ride a bike and save the money that you normally use for your gas expense. If you think about it, this is not really a bad thing but a mere change in lifestyle. In fact, this can even be seen as a healthier lifestyle. Not only can you save more money, but it can also make you much healthier. Not to mention, it can be a very fun experience. Another example is instead of hiring a helper, you might want to be more responsible and clean the house yourself. This will also give you more privacy. As you can see, every change also has its positive side. At the same time, it allows you to earn money. Another example: Instead of using air conditioning, you might just use an electric fan from time to time. After all, a fan is more natural and can significantly lower your expenses. If you are fond of eating several big meals a day, maybe it is time for you to be healthy and go on a diet. Instead of eating and paying for several heavy meals, you might want to order smaller meals. Of course, this is not limited to just yourself, you can include the whole family. You do not just enjoy a healthier life, but you can also save more money. By making simple adjustments, you can effectively lower your costs and save more money. This is important for you to reach your objective of earning at least 6 months of money on savings.

Saving money by lowering your expenses does not always have to give you some form of inconvenience. Many times, it is simply important for you to realize that there are things that you are spending money on that you do not even need. It might just take some time for you to adjust, but it is nonetheless doable. You should learn to prioritize and be responsible. This is also a good way for you to realize that life means so much more than material things and wealth. However, you should not lower your cost to the point that it will give you a hard time. If you cannot make adjustments and lower your cost on one thing, you can just make adjustments on other things.

Saving money can even be fun. It sometimes depends on how you view certain changes. Some people find a better lifestyle when they try to save money. There are those who suddenly learn to appreciate the beauty of minimalism or even frugal living. After all, life itself is also an article, and you have the freedom on how you want to live your life. Just because you have money does not mean that you should live in a certain way. You always have a choice in how you live.

## Saving on housing, transportation, and food expenses

Housing, transportation, and food – these three things normally constitute the biggest part of your expenses, since they are essential to living a good life. With the right attitude and approach, you can also cut down your costs on these things and save more money.

As for the housing, you do not need to live in a big and grand house right away. Such luxury can wait! As long as it has enough room to accommodate you and your family, then that would be fine. You should also be careful in choosing the location. Ideally, your house should be near your place of work. Time is an essential element. Not to mention, if you live far from your place of work, you will have to spend more money on gas. Indeed, time is money so you would not want to waste hours of time just commuting to work. You should train yourself to be productive at all times and increase efficiency.

Before you pay or enter into any contract, negotiate for the best deal. Have several good choices and compare them. When it comes to housing, you need to be very careful as it often involves a big expense.

Regarding transportation, you might want to look for an alternative such walking your way to work or riding a bike. Sometimes it is also better to commute than to bring your own car. This will depend on the circumstances of your situation.

Lowering your expenses is easy, yet it can significantly help you in raising money on savings. This is also something that you can start doing now. So, if you have not done it yet, it is time for you to grab a pen and paper and tally your income and expenses. To be deserving of success, you should make decisions and sacrifices. Do not worry; this is only temporary. When making adjustments, you might experience some inconvenience, especially if you are used to a life where you spend lots of things to bring you comfort. You do not really have to sacrifice your comfort, but you will definitely encounter some uneasiness, especially if you have not yet adjusted to the new routine or set up.

Even though you want to minimize your expenses, take note that this does not mean that you are not allowed to enjoy some luxuries and joys in life. After all, you are still working, and you deserve to have fun. Just be responsible enough, and do not overspend. Always keep your objectives in mind and do everything that you can to succeed.

During this stage, you may have some realizations. Most people learn just how dependent they have been on the comforts that money has to offer. At the same time, they also realize that there are many things that they pay for that they do not actually need. In fact, there are even those who may feel a certain sense of freedom for not being too dependent on money. Indeed, sometimes it is money that can make you feel less free. When a person becomes a slave to money, you end up chasing after it that you forget to notice and appreciate the beauty of life. As the saying goes, "Stop and smell the flowers." By lowering your expenses, you find ways not to depend on money and become free. This is the time when you can stop and finally appreciate life as it is instead of having your mind bombarded with things or services that you have to buy yet you do not actually need. This does not mean that money is bad. Rather, you also need to understand how to spend it wisely. By identifying the things that you actually need from those that you just thought you needed, you can significantly lower your monthly expenses.

It is important to learn to focus and cut down your expenses on these three (housing, transportation, and food) things as they constitute the bulk of your regular expenses. If you can manage these things, then you can have control over your money. Remember never to exceed your means to avoid complications. If necessary, live a simple life. You need to be ready to make some sacrifices to achieve your objective. Do not worry; this is only for a temporary period. Once you reach your objective of having enough savings for 6 months, you can give yourself more flexibility, and it is actually the fruit of your labor since, by then, you can finally live the life that you have always wanted.

Now that you know how to lower your expenses and enjoy more savings effectively, it is time to focus on increasing your income.

DOWNLOAD YOUR FREE BONUS:

**Pursue Your Passion E-book**: Go to- http://bit.ly/PursueYourPassionNow

Go to: bit.ly/PursueYourPassionNow

# Step 2 — Earn More Money

It is time to talk about a very interesting topic, and that is how you can earn more money. The more that you earn, the easier life will be. Discussing how to earn more money is not a strange subject. Almost all people think about how they can earn more, even the rich wants to increase their income. Also, it will be easier for you to reach your 6-month savings that you need if you are able to increase your income. Just be careful not to commit the mistake of also increasing your expenses when your income goes up. Of course, you can treat yourself and increase your expenses a little bit, but be sure to have a good control over it. What you need to focus on is increasing the amount of money that you can save every month. Some people feel even more motivated at this point and further cut down their expenses. Although this is a good thing, remember not to overdo it to the point that your family no longer feels comfortable. Keep in mind that saving money should not make you suffer. Doing simple adjustments should be enough.

When people want to earn money, many of them simply think about money. This is wrong. Instead, you should think about positive actions that you should do that will generate money. Money will not be generated without actions. Rather, you should view money as a product or fruit of something that you did. Hence, the best way to earn money is to think of ways of how you can be of service to people.

If you do this either by selling a product or offering a service, or even both, then you will be paid in money. This is how you actually make money. As you can see, it is different from simply thinking about money. If you want to earn money, then you should take actions and work for it.

Earning more money is actually what so many people want. From time to time, people wonder: How can I earn more money? This is also the reason why there are people who want to escape from their 9-5 job. This is true especially when they realize that their 9-5 job, secured as it may be, also limits their earning potential. When you have the usual office job, generally, you already know just how much you will earn in a month, even in a year. There is a fixed amount that you will get for all of your efforts. But, when you freelance or put up your own business, even if it is just an online business, you create an opportunity to earn more income, and the good news here is that there is no limit to how much you can earn. Of course, there are different ways to earn more money. Some may involve a simple increase in your current income from your job, yet it could still be very helpful to your current situation, while others might be riskier but with a higher earning potential.

So, how can you effectively increase your income and earn more money? Let us discuss the different ways that you can do to make this happen:

## Get a promotion or a raise (even if you do not want to leave your job)

To boost your income, the most natural way would be to focus on the work that you already have. Take note that this does not mean that you should stick to your job, but at least use it to reach your objective of getting enough savings for six months. Do your best and try to get promoted. As you may already know, promotions are associated with an increase in the salary. Another option that you have is to talk with your boss and politely ask for a raise, if your boss is understanding enough, you can even explain your situation to him, and he might help you out. However, keep in mind that your boss is not obliged to give you a raise unless there are compelling legal reasons to do so; therefore, you should also learn to manage your expectations.

Of course, before you can expect to be promoted or given a raise, you should first deserve it. This is why you need to do your best at work, even if it is the work that you want to abandon later on. Still, it does not change the fact that at the present time, it is your current work that allows you to pay for the bills.

Learn the skills that your career teaches you. They may be useful in other things other than your current work. The work experience itself is also a rich source of knowledge. When you are used to working hard, then other kinds of work can soon be easy for you to do.

You have to understand that just because you want to change your job does not mean that you can just abandon your present work immediately. In fact, it may mean doing more on your present job to allow you to shift to a new job. You first need to have a strong foundation before you can safely take on a new route. This is important especially when other people depend on you for support. The good news is that it is something that *you* can do. It may just take more time and effort, but it is nonetheless doable, and you are the right person to make it happen.

## Freelance (after hours of using the skills from your career)

Your present career will arm you with certain skills. These days, freelancing is getting popular. No, you do not need to leave your job and be a full-time freelancer. Although this is possible and there are people out there who have reported success by going freelancer on a full-time basis, it is still quite a risky venture, so you need to be careful with your decisions and actions. What you can do is to be a part-time freelancer. If you work during the day, you might want to handle some freelancer projects in the evening or over the weekends. One of the best things about freelancing is that you get to be in control of your time. Take note that just because you have more control of your time when you are a freelancer does not mean that you can just be lazy. Rather, you have to spend your time effectively and efficiently.

Freelancing is a good way to get more work, which means more money. If you are serious about boosting your present income, then this is definitely something that you might want to try.

Freelancing is fun. In fact, it is not unusual to find someone who simply tried freelancing but ended up doing it as the full-time job. Working as a freelancer gives you the opportunity to be your own boss and to set your own hours. You can even choose the client or projects that you want to work on. However, the challenge here is that you will be living from paycheck to paycheck. This means that if you stop working or if you run out of projects to work on, then you will also not get any income.

**Start an online business: Kindle Publishing, blogging, affiliate marketing, etc.**

Another thing that you can do is to engage in an online business. There are many people these days who are able to leave their day job and work full time in the comfort of their homes because of their online business. This is a good way for you to earn extra and passive income. In addition, this can be a fun activity that you can do after your office work. Since it simply involves an online presence, you can engage in this kind of business even in the comfort of your home. Now, there are many kinds of online business. Let us look at notable ways to earn money online:

> ➢ Kindle Publishing

This is one of the best ways to earn passive income online. You can write ebooks and publish them on Kindle. The ebooks will be sold at Amazon and other key book retailers online. What is an ebook? It is an electronic or digital format of a book; hence, it is called an *e-book*. Record shows that ebook sales on Amazon have now become higher than sales from traditionally published paperback books. Today, more and more people are learning to appreciate the value and benefits of using an ebook over a paperback book, such as being able to bring and access your ebooks anywhere you go, to avoid wear and tear, easy search feature, and others.

Some people have earned a high amount of income just by publishing ebooks. For publishing on Amazon, you might want to use KDP or Kindle Direct Publishing. This is the publishing platform of Amazon. When you publish using KDP, you get to distribute your ebooks not only to Amazon but also to other ebook channels. Why Amazon? Well, different cases show that Amazon has the biggest share in terms of ebook sales. This is because Amazon has well established itself in the market with millions of loyal and active customers. If you write good ebooks, you will definitely have a market for your product.

You can also come up with a physical, paperback copy of your ebooks by going to *Createspace*. Createspace is also owned by Amazon. It is the publishing platform that will allow you to do publish your book in a paperback format. It is also worth noting that both KDP and Createspace are free to use.

So, just how much can you make? Well, there are no hard and fast rules on this matter. There are ebook sellers out there who barely earn anything, while there are also those who earn thousands of dollars, and even a fortune, from their ebooks. You should approach this as a business where your ebook is your product.

Now, a common problem that people face when they use this approach is that they are not confident of their writing. After all, before you can have an ebook that you can sell, you need to write a book. This is easy if you are fond of writing, but what if you are one of the many people out there who simply have no interest or time to write? Well, do not worry; this may surprise you, but the truth is that there are many ebook sellers out there who do not write. How is this possible? The way to do this is to hire a ghostwriter to write your book. A ghostwriter will do the work of writing your book for you. When you hire a ghostwriter, you remain as the sole author of the book. Your ghostwriter will not have any credit as long as you pay him to write your book. You can find affordable ghostwriting services from content mills like Upwork or Freelancer. However, just a word of caution: Stay away from ghostwriters that offer their services for a very low price as they tend to have low-quality work as well. Now, the ghostwriting rates vary greatly. You can find a ghostwriter to write your book for $200, but there are also those who would charge thousands of dollars for their service. If you want a highly professional quality of work, then you might want to pay for a more experienced ghostwriter. However, expect the fee to be higher than usual. To make money out of selling ebooks, you do not really need to hire a highly professional ghostwriter. You can stick to ghostwriters that will charge a few hundred dollars for a book. The important thing is to have a work that has a decent quality.

You may not be aware of this, but more than 60% of published books are written by ghostwriters. Some of the books in the bestsellers list were also made by professional ghostwriters. When it comes to the business of making money by selling ebooks, you will find that hiring several ghostwriters to write ebooks for you can be helpful. However, you should be careful with your budget. Be sure to manage your money properly. You can start with a few books and see how they work.

People say that you should not judge a book by its cover. If you are serious about making money by selling ebooks, you should understand that people do judge books by their cover, or at least having a beautiful cover can draw more attention to your book, which can increase sales. Make sure that every ebook that you sell has a beautiful book cover. If you do not know how to make your own cover, you might want to hire people from *Fiverr* to do the work for you. You can get your book cover for just $5 (per book).

Now, once you have your ebook ready and complete, then you now have a product that you can sell. A nice thing about an ebook is that it has unlimited supply without you having to spend anything. Once you have your ebook, then it is with you forever, and people can buy as many copies as they want. Hence, only the initial cost can be quite high (if you hire a ghostwriter), but then after that, you will have a product that you can sell as many times as you can at no cost on your part.

Okay, having a product is one thing, being able to sell it is another. Another important part of this business is marketing your ebook/s. There are many ways to do this. You can use social media, your blog, guest post on authority sites, and others. You should try to market your ebook as much as you can. Keep in mind that even if you have a wonderful product to sell, you cannot expect for it to generate profits if the market is not aware that your product even exists. You should promote your ebook. This is another reason why you should make sure that your ebook has a good quality. If you know that it has a bad quality, then you will have a hard time promoting it.

Quality is important. You simply cannot expect an ebook that has a poor quality to sell and generate a decent amount of profits. If you offer an ebook that has a bad quality, it will most likely end up with lots of negative reviews. In any kind of business, as well as when you are selling anything, quality is very important.

But, when it comes to an ebook, what exactly makes a work of high or at least good quality? Well, the book has to be able to satisfy the wants or needs of its readers. If it is a non-fiction book, then it has to provide the readers with useful information on the subject. It should also respect the basic rules on grammar and punctuation. It should relay the information in an easy to understand manner. It should also be properly formatted. Presentation is another important thing. Hence, it should have a catchy and interesting cover to draw more attention to the book, among other things. The more that you exert efforts to create a good book, the easier you will be able to sell it, and this means higher profits.

Making money by selling ebooks can be a highly rewarding venture. When you take this approach, you should learn to consider it as a business and not just a passion for writing and sharing your work. At present, the ebook industry is also competitive. Every day, new ebooks are being published. Still, it remains to be a lucrative business. You might have to publish several books before you can start to appreciate the flow of income. Although it is possible to have success with just one book, experts suggest that you can more effectively increase your sales by having more books for sale. You might want to try different genres and see which one works best for you. Another way that is recommended is to conduct your own research and analysis of the market and see the kind of books that sell. You can then write a book that relates to the latest trend. This way you will know that there is an existing market and demand for your ebook.

If you want to have a decent flow of passive income, then selling ebooks is definitely one of the best choices that you can make.

Instead of selling on Amazon and other online retailers, you also have an option to sell directly from your own website or blog. This way, you will enjoy full control of everything. It is also a good way to earn a higher income per sale. However, you will also be responsible for everything, such as in promoting your ebooks, processing payments, and others.

The key to Kindle publishing success is to produce high-quality books and publish as many books as you can. Both quality and quantity are important. You also need a strong marketing arm to be able to promote your products (ebooks) effectively. Indeed, many people have made a fortune by selling ebooks on Amazon and on other online bookstores. You might also want to use various pen names depending on the genre of your books. Of course, you are also free to use your real name if you want. Indeed, when it comes to making money online, selling ebooks is something that has been proven to be a good way to make lots of money.

> Blogging

Blogging is another popular way to earn money online. There are many blogs out there that earn thousands and even millions of dollars. What is a blog? Well, a blog is like a digital diary or journal that is shared with the world. Blogs are so famous that you can think of anything topic that you want and you will surely find related blogs out there somewhere just by doing a search online. It should be noted that the blog itself does not make money, but what you do with it can allow you to generate a nice income. A common way to earn money from your blog is through the use of ads. This is where ads will be posted on your blog, and you can earn every time a visitor clicks on the ads and/or per 1,000 views. There are many ad programs out there, but the one that is most recommended is Google AdSense. This is what professional bloggers use. And, since it is owned by Google, you can rest for sure that you can trust it. However, unlike other ad programs, it is not that easy to be qualified to be part of the Google AdSense programs. You first need to send an application to Google, and it should allow you to post Google ads on your blog. Although many bloggers have a hard time to get approved, it is worth noting that if you know the right steps, then you can easily be approved to post Google ads. Here are notable points that you should know:

o   Regular traffic

Before you even send your application to Google, you should first establish regular traffic to your blog. It does not have to be a huge traffic, but you should at least have regular blog visitors. Hence, you will have to spend a few weeks or months working on your blog before you apply for Google AdSense. Getting regular traffic to your blog or site might be a real challenge in the beginning. But, just stick to the best practices, and you will soon establish your own traffic and a good following online.

o   Contents

Your blog should already have some contents. Otherwise, Google will most likely not approve your application. There are no hard and fast rules as to how many posts you should have on your blog, but it is suggested that it should have at least 20 quality posts to have a good chance of being approved for the AdSense program.

Having contents on your blog will also help Google to identify what your blog is about. This is important to know the kind of ads that will be displayed on your blog.

o   Quality

Last but not least, make sure that your blog has a good quality; otherwise, Google will definitely not approve your application. What you need is a good-quality blog. This means that your blog should be presentable and professional. It must also have decent contents and a good following. It does not have to be a perfect blog but at least make it presentable enough. Do not make it hard for Google to approve your blog. The more that you are able to establish your blog the higher is your chances of being approved by Google.

When it comes to blogging, one very important element that you should know is SEO. SEO stands for search engine optimization. This refers to how visible and discoverable your blog is on the Internet. Ideally, your blog should be on the first page of a search result. However, this can be quite challenging considering the level of competition and number of blogs in the market. With the help of SEO, you can increase your online visibility. This is important since no matter how amazing your blog is, you cannot expect for it to generate any decent traffic if it is hard to find online. Indeed, without the use of effective SEO, it is impossible to generate decent and regular traffic to your blog. Let us now discuss important SEO techniques that you should know:

➢ Long-tail keywords

When it comes to SEO, the number one thing that you should know is how to use keywords. Gone are the days when you can just use any keywords that you want. Today, you need to learn to use long-tail keywords. These keywords are composed of at least three targeted words to help increase the visibility of a particular blog post. Needless to say, it should be related to the blog post that you are promoting. For example, if you manage a business blog, do not just use the word *business* as your keywords. Instead, use long-tail keywords like *how to trade goods from Alaska* or any other related long-tail keywords. It also helps to make it specific. Also, remember that long-tail keywords should be composed of at least three words. Now, the next concern would be identifying the keywords that you should use. After all, there are countless of keywords that you can come up, so how do you know which keywords have a market? The way to do this is to use a keywords checker. Many bloggers recommend using Google Keyword Planner. With Google Keyword Planner, you will be able to tell how many times certain keywords or keyword phrase is searched for online. It will also give you suggestions of other keywords that you can use. To be able to access the Google Keyword Planner, you should have an AdWords account.

Google AdWords is a Google program that will allow you to post ads. This is different from AdSense where you allow other people to post ads on your blog. With AdSense, you are the one who is posting ads. Do not worry; you do not need to post ads. If you just want to use the Keywords Planner, then you can do so without having to pay for anything. Once you have an AdSense account, then you can have access to Google Keyword Planner. Picking the right keywords is important as it will significantly help you increase the blog's traffic. When it comes to any online business, getting good traffic is important as this allows you to get customers or buyers. Indeed, when it comes to SEO, the use of keywords tops the list.

➢ Keyword density

You also need to observe the right keyword density. What is keyword density? It simply refers to the number of times that your keywords are repeated in the article. Years ago, you can easily appear on the first page of search engines by repeating your chosen keywords many times. However, search engines have already developed and now ensure that those that appear on the first pages of the SERP (search engine results pages) have good quality. Hence, you cannot just fill your content with keywords. In fact, filling your content with keywords is now known as keyword stuffing which is not considered a good practice. When a search engine detects that you are involved in the practice of keyword stuffing, it will give your content a lower SEO ranking, which makes it less visible to search engines. As you can see, it is important that you observe the right keyword density to avoid search engines from thinking that you are engaged in keyword stuffing. So, what is the right keyword density? There is no strict rule on this matter yet. However, various expert bloggers agree that a good keyword density would be around 3%-5%. This refers to the number of times that your keywords should appear in your article.

You should also avoid the practice of forcing to repeat your keywords in an article. The keywords should flow smoothly in the article that your readers will barely notice that you even use keywords. Pay attention to the flow of the article. Take note that the use of keywords is only a part of your posting. The more important part is to provide quality information that your readers will enjoy and find helpful.

> Share

You have to share your content. Even if you come up with a good post, you cannot just rely on search engines to find and promote your content. It is your job to market and promote what you have posted. Do not worry; this is not difficult to do. A good and effective way to do this is by sharing your content on social media. When it comes to sharing, social media is your number one solution. However, you should take note that you must first have something that is worth sharing. You would not want to irritate your followers and connections with senseless and low-quality posts. So, once you have a content that you are proud of, something that you know that your target readers will find useful, then you can tap the power of social media to reach a bigger market.

One of the best things about social media is that those who like your content can share it with their own network. Do you realize its potential? This means that every time a person shares your content, you get to tap with a new set of network. Now, just imagine what will happen if many of these people like and share your content. This is actually how a content gets viral online. But, of course, for this to happen, you should ensure that you have something that is worth sharing. Make sure that every post that you make gives value to your readers. Once again, quality has to be your number one priority.

Indeed, when you engage in blogging, SEO is one thing that you should focus on. With high-quality contents and the right SEO strategy, you can be a successful blogger.

Blogging is definitely one of the best and is the most popular way to make money online. It is also a way to establish your expertise on a particular subject, provided that you are able to post useful information. Even today, some people earn a full-time income working as a blogger.

➢ Affiliate marketing

Another way to earn money online is through affiliate marketing. What is affiliate marketing? It is where you sell the products of other people. You then earn a share (income) every time a person purchases the product that you promote. When you work as an affiliate, you will be given an *affiliate link*. This is the link that you give to your readers. They can buy the product that you promote through this link. When a person buys a product through this link, then you will get your cut or share from the sale. This is how you earn money as an affiliate. Now, there are also programs that will reward you with a small fee every time your affiliate link gets clicked even if a sale is not consummated. Still, if you want to earn a decent income by being an affiliate marketer, your aim is to make your readers buy the product that you promote via your affiliate link.

If you want to be a successful affiliate marketer, then you need to establish your presence online. It is strongly advised that you put up a nice blog. Now, a common mistake is to oversell a product. Although your objective is to be able to sell something, you should know that overselling a product can be bad for your reputation. One thing that you should focus on is building trust with your readers. Take note that it is hard, if not impossible, to build trust when the readers know that you will make money from them. Gone are the days when you can just promote something and expect for people to be fooled easily and click on your affiliate link. When you work as an affiliate marketer, you need to work on establishing trust. After all, you cannot expect a person to buy from your link if he does not even trust you.

So, how can you gain the trust of your readers? Well, you need to give them value. This means that you should tell them the truth. Never lie to your readers. If there is something bad about a particular product, then be open and honest about it. Your readers will appreciate it if you are honest. After all, people do not expect for any product to be completely perfect. In fact, if you do not know any negative thing about a particular product, then chances are that you probably do not know it that much yet.

By doing a simple search online, you will find lots of affiliate programs. You can choose whether you want to use multiple affiliate programs or simply focus on a single program. One of the most successful affiliate programs is *Clickbank*.

It is up to you if you want to promote a particular product. Just avoid making it look like you just want to be able to sell the product. You should consider that your readers want to know the pros and cons of buying a product. He does not read your content to be encouraged to buy something. Instead, he is being careful. Do not make him buy something that you know will only make him disappointed. Doing so will only make you lose your customers.

You might want to come up with a review website. You can also make an honest comparison of competing products. The important thing is to give valuable information to your readers.

So, just how much can you make? Well, many successful affiliate marketers earn thousands of dollars every month. There are those who work as an affiliate marketer on a full-time basis. Unfortunately, if you do not give it enough focus and efforts, you might end up like other affiliate marketers who barely make any income. But, do not worry; with the right approach and hard work, you can make your affiliate marketing experience a pleasant and fruitful one. It just really takes time to establish yourself as an affiliate marketer, especially in the beginning. Just persist, and you will soon be able to reap the fruits of your labor.

It is also advised that you establish your online presence in social media. Successful affiliate marketers know how effective social media is. When it comes to gaining traffic and exposure, then the power of social media can be harnessed.

You might want to focus on a particular niche, but you can also come up with a site that reviews various products. It is recommended that you review products that you understand. For example, if you are personally interested and knowledgeable in computers, then you might want to write blog posts about various computer products. You can also make comparisons of the latest models from different brands. Of course, this is just an example. There is actually no limit on how you want to approach affiliate marketing.

Since you will earn a particular percentage from every sale, it means that a product that has a higher price will most likely give you a higher profit. However, this does not mean that there is no money for products that have a low price. When you market a product that has a low price, the key is to make sales by the volume. It is easy for people to buy cheap products, but they tend to be more careful before they purchase expensive products.

So, is it for you? If you are fond of making product reviews, then you might enjoy working as an affiliate marketer. It is worth repeating that to be successful, you need to establish trust. To do this, you should provide your audience with true and helpful information regarding the product that you are marketing.

There are many other ways to earn money online. This is because the online world connects you with people, and these people can be your customers/clients. Indeed, if you want to increase your income, you should definitely look into putting up your own online business. Another advantage of running an online business is that it allows you to connect to a big market. When you have an online presence, the whole world becomes your potential market. It is just a matter of pulling the right strings and positioning yourself properly. Although it may take some time to establish your presence online, it is nonetheless doable and is very much worth it.

# Step 3 — Learn a High Income Producing Skill

If your income is still not enough, or if you simply want to further increase your earning capacity so you can quickly achieve your objective of having 6 months of savings, then you should learn a high income producing skill. This way, you can have a higher income per month. Although it is true that you can make money regardless of the kind of work that you do, it is also true that there are certain work or work positions that simply get a much higher pay than others. However, such positions usually require technical knowledge. The good news is that you do not have to enroll in a formal class just to learn them. You can learn these skills by reading from books or even just by doing a diligent research online. Let us take a look at some of these key work positions that can significantly give your income a boost:

- Digital marketing: PPC manager, social media marketing, web design

All these deal with the online world. Indeed, digital marketing is very important for businesses these days. If a business does not have an online presence, then you can expect that it is probably far behind the competition. If you can learn digital marketing, then there is a demand for what you can do. You do not have to learn the whole aspect of digital marketing. If you want, you can just specialize on a particular subject. For example, as a PPC manager, you will have to deal with advertisements. PPC stands for *pay per click*. It is where you buy visits to your site or blog by posting ads online instead of merely relying on search engines to find and display your site. As a PPC manager, you will have to run and monitor ads and make sure that the ads are able to promote the site or blog effectively. You need to be able to target your market properly to increase your chances of turning visitors into actual conversions (sales, sign-ups, or whatever your objective might be). You also need to be able to write short yet compelling ads, among others. Indeed, the job of a PPC marketer is also quite challenging, but it is nonetheless learnable. If you give it enough time and effort, you will surely be able to master the ins and outs of PPC advertising, and businesses will definitely want to work with you.

Social media marketing is another very hot service today. If you can promote something online effectively, then many businesses and people would want to work with you. Considering how helpful and important social media is, people spend money just to establish their presence online. But, of course, to be able to market something effectively through social media, you need to have a strong presence and quality following first. The good news is that once you have established yourself, then there are a lot of things that you can do, and this opens the gate to opportunities to make a nice profit.

- Web design

The design of one's site or blog can make a difference. Many times, the design alone separates professional blogs and sites from unprofessional ones. If you learn web design and get good at it, you can charge a premium price for your services. Indeed, many businesses pay a high price just to have someone to design their website. If you have an eye for the right designs and combination of colors, then this is probably the job for you. Professional web designers normally charge thousands of dollars per project. This is also something that you can do on the side while you keep your regular job.

Having a professionally-designed blog or site is important to any business. If a particular site is poorly designed, then chances are that people will also not take it seriously. If people do not treat you seriously, then you cannot expect to earn any decent income. As a web designer, you are going to help people and businesses attract their market with your catchy and grabbing web designs. If you ever take this approach, prepare to learn some computer coding.

- Programming

Since we live in the age of computers and the Internet, it is clear that programming is considered to be highly essential. There is simply a high demand for programmers. After all, everything that happens and exists online depends on programming. If you know how to program properly, then you are a key asset in any online business. The good news is that you do not need to take any formal study to be a good programmer. There are many books, including free books online, that will teach you how to program effectively. Although programming can be considered a highly technical field, it is also something where you can earn a high pay. Again, there is a huge demand for programmers. The truth is that every blog or site requires application of programming. Hence, not only will you be able to earn a good income as a programmer, but you are assured that there will always be a continuing demand for your services.

There are also many videos on YouTube that will teach you the basics of programming. If you are not that knowledgeable when it comes to computers, you might find it very challenging to understand even the basic codes. However, do not be discouraged. Coding is actually simpler than you might think. If you give it enough time and effort, you can be a good programmer.

- High-Ticket Sales

This is about selling expensive products online, usually belonging to other people like businesses. This works just like affiliate marketing but can be more challenging in the sense that people tend to be more careful with spending their money when it comes to expensive things. However, despite the challenge, this can be a highly lucrative career where you can earn lots of money even from a single transaction. There are people out there who make a living and earn lots of money solely from high-ticket sales.

When you take this route, you definitely need to establish a good rapport with your customers. Hence, you need to establish trust. Needless to say, the way to do this is to give value. If you want to focus on high-ticket sales, it is strongly advised that you put up a professional blog. This is the way for you to gain the trust of your audience. Some people try to be successful simply by focusing on social media, but it is not considered the best approach. Of course, social media is still important, especially in terms of sharing your work and reaching a bigger market, but the way to connect with your potential buyers and be able to earn their trust is by putting up your own blog or site and posting helpful contents.

It is also worth noting that high-ticket sales should not just be about making a successful sale. Just like with affiliate marketing, you need to focus more on building a good relationship with people. You need to earn their trust. This is the way to have a continuous business. You would not want to gamble and lose everything just for one sale. As long as you stick to the right practices and are able to build a good relationship, then sales will follow on their own. But, if you become too greedy and be concerned with how you can earn money than helping people by providing useful information, then it would be difficult even to consummate a single high-ticket sale.

- Freelance writing

When it comes to making money online, freelance writing is always on the list. In fact, majority of the people who earn money online are related to freelance writing. This is easy to understand since every website or blog needs contents. Not to mention, blogs need a continuous supply of fresh contents to keep it active. So, if you want to earn nice income online, then you should definitely try freelance writing online.

So, how much do freelance writers make? Well, the price varies. Those who are just starting out and are still learning how to write earn a few dollars per article, but if you get good at it, you can earn hundreds of dollars for a single article.

Beginning freelance writers normally start with content mills like Upwork or Freelancer. However, if you want to earn a good amount of income, it should be noted that going to content mills is not your best option. They are only good if you just want to practice writing but not to earn a good income. However, as an exception, you might find good-paying clients from content mills although the chances are slim. If you want to earn a decent amount of income by freelance writing, you should send your work directly to publishers that pay for freelance work. There are many sites, and blogs out there that accept pitches and works from freelance and they would pay you for accepted pieces. If you freelance to authority sites, you can earn a decent amount per article. If you write for content mills, the usual rate is just a poor $3 per 500-word article. You can compare that to writing for established sites that pay on average at least $60 per article, and the price can go even much higher. So, if you think you have a good way with words or if you are willing to give yourself through time and practice, then you can definitely earn a nice income by freelance writing alone. In fact, there are people out there who earn a living solely through freelance writing.

There is a huge demand for people who can write high-quality articles. Businesses are also willing to pay a premium price for excellent writers. However, it should be noted that writing is a skill and an art. You cannot just expect for your work to be accepted for publication if you do not know how to write effectively. However, do not be disheartened; the truth is that writing can be learned. As long as you are willing to give it enough time to practice and study it, then you can significantly improve your writing over time.

When you work as a freelance writer, you need to learn how to write pitches. A pitch is a letter that is normally directed to an editor where you pitch a story (article) that you will provide. Take note that this is not just about telling the editor what you want to write, but you should also show why it is a good piece for the publishing house, as well as why you are the right person to write it.

However, before you write your pitch letter, there are certain things that you need to take note of. The first thing that you want to know is if the website or blog accepts pitches or works from freelance writers. Normally, you'll know about this by checking the editorial section of the site, if any. If there are none, you can simply send a message via the site's *Contact Us* page. Once your pitch letter is accepted, the editor will tell you if you can commence with writing the article. You may have to prepare to do some revisions. Normally, you will be paid after your work is finally accepted for publication.

As a freelance writer, you can write to multiple publishers. In fact, this is actually how freelance writers normally make money. The more sites and blogs that you write for, the higher potential income will be. It is also not unusual for a freelance writer to get some sort of regular work from a client. This happens when a client is happy with your work. Hence, it is always important to focus on the quality of your work.

Indeed, freelance writing can be a highly lucrative career. There are people out there who are able to leave their day job and just freelance full time in the comfort of their homes without a boss to please. But, of course, this does not mean that you will have fewer responsibilities. Although you have no boss to please, you will now have clients and editors to work with. Being your own boss also means being responsible for everything. If you stop writing from too long, then the flow of income will also stop. This is one of the challenges faced by freelance writers. However, if you are personally fond of writing, then you may find this path to be very rewarding and highly enjoyable.

- Ghostwriting

This is another branch of freelance writing. However, unlike freelance writing where you normally keep the byline, you will not receive any credit when you work as a ghostwriter. As a ghostwriter, you write something for a client and not earn any credit for the work. You will only be paid for your work, but you will not claim any ownership over the work. It is the client who owns your work. It is noteworthy to that majority of published books are made by ghostwriters. Since you will not claim any ownership or credit over the work, you can charge a much higher fee than doing a typical freelance writing job. Professional ghostwriters earn more than $10,000 per book. In fact, it is not unusual for professional ghostwriters to charge more than $20,000 per book. Indeed, working as a ghostwriter can be a highly lucrative career. There are also simple and small-time ghostwriting projects that you can take where you can earn a few hundred dollars for writing a short book. This is not bad at all especially if you just want to earn something to pay the bills or simply to practice your writing skills, as well as while you are waiting for a big project to come. Some freelance writers end up working as a full-time ghostwriter. The term ghostwriter is usually associated with ghostwriting books, but it is worth noting that ghostwriting is not limited to writing books. As a ghostwriter, you can also ghostwrite articles, blog posts, brochures and manuals, poems, and even song lyrics. It is all about doing something where someone else is going to take the credit for your work. For this reason, ghostwriters are able to charge a much higher amount than the usual.

Another interesting thing about working as a ghostwriter is the upfront fees. When you work as a book ghostwriter, you can ask your client for an upfront fee which can be as high as 50% or even 60% (or even higher) of the total price. This is something that you will discuss and negotiate with your client. This is normal in ghostwriting. After all, you will be writing a book, and it will most likely take time for you to finish it. Hence, it is just right to ask for an upfront fee. The said fee can also act as some form of acceptance fee, as well as for your security as you work on the project. After all, it would be an unlikely situation to start working carefully on a client's book without being sure if the client would even pay you.

There are professional ghostwriters out there who make a fine living just by ghostwriting books. If you enjoy writing books, then this is definitely something that you should consider. Just remember that when you work as a ghostwriter, you do not get any credit for your work. Your work belongs to your client as if the client was the one who wrote it.

# Step 4 — Get a Freelance or Part-Time Job Using Your New Skill

Now that you have a new skill whether from your current work or on your own, you can now use it to make more money. The way to do this is to get a part-time freelance job using your new skill. This is definitely an effective way to supplement your income and make more money. Every new skill can be used for something where you can get paid. What people often overlook is that there is something that they can do to make a nice profit. Now, once you know you are ready to offer your skill to others, it is time to make people know about it. You cannot expect for work to appear just out of nowhere. You need to market your expertise; otherwise, you will have trouble with finding any clients.

So, how do you promote your service? Again, the best way to do this is to have a website or a blog, you can then use the power of social media to help spread the word about what you do. The more people you reach through your site and social media promotions, the higher is your chance to get clients. Since you will not be quitting your day job, you should make it clear that you will only render freelance work part-time. When you are just starting out, it is not really advised that you quit your day job right away. Freelancing is like a business. You cannot expect to make profits from it right away. It will also take time to establish yourself in the market. So, to be safe, do not quit your usual job and jump into freelancing full time right away. You need to be careful with your decisions, especially if there are people who depend on you for support. Do not worry; the important thing is that there is progress and that you are moving forward.

- Improve your skills and create connections in the industry

You cannot just be content with your present skills. Continuous improvement has to be a constant priority. It does not matter whether you work as a marketer, a writer, programmer, or whatever position you take, there is always something that you can do to be better. You should not overlook the existing competition between and among freelancers. These days, many people are turning to freelance jobs, so you should definitely give this and its implications some considerations, especially with respect to how it can affect your business.

Another thing that you can do is to improve your connections in the industry that you engage in. By building useful connections, you can have more flow of work, and this means more income. Who knows, you might even reach the point where you can totally leave your day job and work as a freelancer full time. This way, you can have more control over your time and your life.

A good way to build connections is by using LinkedIn. LinkedIn is a social media platform just like Facebook. However, the key difference is that LinkedIn is a social media platform specially made for professionals. This is where you can get key contacts of people who might be related to your business and could help you with your business. However, do not forget that it is still just a social media platform; hence, do not expect so much from it. It is still you who needs to do the hard work. Still, if used effectively, you can tap this social media channel to propel your business by connecting with the right people.

It is also good to use LinkedIn to allow you to meet and connect with influencers. Influencers are people who are considered as experts in their field of knowledge, and they often have a quality following. Take note that this refers to quality following and not just the number of followers or connections that an influencer has. Quality connections refer to people who would actually engage in what you share. Unfortunately, there are also people who simply ignore what their connections share with them. So, why do you want to connect with an influencer? Well, just imagine what can happen if an influencer supports and promotes your posts? You can effectively draw a huge market, which means more clients or customers. So, how do you make an influencer promote your work? Well, the number one thing that you need is to have something that is worthy of being promoted, something that an influencer would also find interesting and helpful. Now, you can simply connect with an influencer of LinkedIn by sending him/her a connection request. If it gets accepted, then you will be finally connected. In which case, you can now send him a direct message. This is where you will get to communicate directly with an influencer and maybe ask him to help you. Of course, an influencer is not obliged to support you. The best way to convince an influencer to help you is by making him see that you are also valuable. The best way to do this is to provide useful and interesting contents. If an influencer sees that you are really serious about what you do and that you are good at it, then he will most likely respond to your messages and even work with you. Take note that it is also not uncommon for an influencer to charge you for helping promote you online.

Of course, LinkedIn is not the only way to establish more connections. You can also use and distribute business cards. You can also make use of email signatures to help promote your business. You can even use the usual social media channel like Facebook to establish more connections. The important thing is to make people know about what you offer and be able to establish a connection with them.

Another network that you should establish comes from referrals from your own clients. In fact, this one is very important. Through referrals alone, there is a chance that you can have a well-established business. This is another reason why you should ensure that you render work of high quality. Your clients cannot refer you to another if they are not satisfied with your work. Hence, the quality of your work should always be your main priority. You should also keep your clients on your contact list. It is also advised that you message them every now and then even just to ask how they are doing. This is how you maintain a good relationship. Do not be discouraged if a client could not hire or give you more work today, you may not know when you might need him in the future.

It should also be noted that there is no end to improving one's skills. If you think that you have already learned everything that is to know about a particular job position, then try to compare yourself with your competitors in the industry and identify your strengths and weaknesses. Take note that your strengths and weaknesses are relative to the strengths and weaknesses of your competitors. You can also branch out and learn other related skills. The important thing is to always keep on making progress and improvements. Improving one's skill is a never-ending journey. This is also why it is advised that you just enjoy the learning process and do not rush it. It will not end anyway, so there is nothing much for you to worry about. The important thing is to keep on learning and improving.

- Increase your income and build confidence

As you continue to engage in this kind of work, you will learn ways to further increase your income. Also, as you get more projects done, you will have more confidence in yourself. This will come over time as you get used to your acquired skill.

At the beginning of your career, you might not have enough confidence in yourself. This is because you are still unaware of what you can do. This is true, especially if you know that you still have not mastered the skill involved in the service that you offer. However, as you gain more experience, you will also gain more confidence. This is also the skill and confidence that you need to be able to take on bigger projects.

When you are just starting out, you might be tempted to hit a big project right away. Although this can be an opportunity to make big money, you should be sure that you can handle the task properly. If the skill required is something that you are not that confident in, then you might want to start out with small yet decent projects. This is a good way to gain more experience and confidence in what you can do.

As you gain more confidence and as you further develop your skill, you can start to charge higher rates. Of course, this means that you should also target the right market – those who can pay.

Something that you should realize is that opportunities come from other people. Hence, if you want to have more opportunities to earn money like getting new projects with a higher pay, then you need to reach out and connect with the right people. Now, when it comes to connecting to people, many would advise the use of social media. However, you should not overlook the reach of your own blog or website. If you set it up properly with the right SEO techniques, then you will also have your own network from your site. This network will most probably be composed of people who are interested in the service that you offer.

It is possible for you to grow your income significantly to the point that you will feel as if you could leave your job and just work full time as a freelancer. In fact, this is how people become full-time freelancers. In the beginning, they think that it is just a way to supplement their income until they realize that they could earn so much more money if they work as a full-time freelancer. Normally, this happens once you have established a good client base that you are assured a regular flow of projects.

## Should you work as a full-time freelancer?

If your freelance business succeeds, you will definitely reach a point where you will be asking yourself if you should just leave your office work and just work as a full-time time freelancer as you try to reach your objective of getting enough savings for 6 months. Well, this is something that you need to decide on carefully. You need to weigh the consequences of leaving your job. Is your freelancing business enough to support itself? Do you get a consistent flow of freelance projects? How long do you think will you be able to maintain it? Think about and analyze every detail to be sure of your decision. Indeed, leaving your secured 9-5 job and becoming a full-time freelancer can be a life-changing experience that you need to consider carefully. This is something that only you can answer. The important thing is to be completely honest with yourself as you come up with a firm decision.

If you can reach your objective without leaving your secured 9-5 job, then perhaps it is safer for you to just be more patient until you achieve your objective. This way, you are sure that you do not have to take any risks. However, if you are more of the adventurous type and if you think that your freelance business can now support itself, then you might want to become a full-time freelancer.

If you feel the freelance business is also the dream job that you have always wanted, then that is really good for you. However, you can also do freelancing just for the sake of increasing your income, which is not a bad thing. After all, there is an objective that you need to accomplish, and being able to raise enough savings to support you and your family for 6 months is not a joke. In fact, it might take you more than a year to do it. This is why you have to exert all efforts to be able to do it as quickly as possible.

Continuity of business is important. If your freelance or online business will only give you a decent income for a few months only, then it is not safe to quit your regular job. Just like any other business, an online business or a freelance business has to be well established. While you are still setting it up, you cannot rely on it completely. If you have a family to support and a mortgage to worry about, you definitely would not want to take too much risk.

You have to be objective when it comes to analyzing your business. Pay attention to how much it actually makes than how much you think it could make. Although it is good to exercise positive thinking, you should still learn to recognize the hard facts and problems that you might be facing. To be safe, it might be the best option for you not to quit your job even if you are confident that your freelance or online business would be enough to support your needs. The key is to quit your job only when you are certain that what you have now is enough. There are two things that you need: a 6-month savings and a side income that also makes good money. Take note that although it is referred to as a side income, it does not mean that it does not earn well. It should, if possible, be as good or nearly as good as your current income source.

You do not always have to manage an online business or a freelance business. You also have a choice to just apply to another company or simply get another work other than your normal 9-5 work. Just do not make it too hard. Remember that you will only need it to supplement your current income. Hence, if you are really not into the use of computers, then you might want to take other kinds of work relevant to your skill. For example, if your current job relates to health and nutrition, you might want to work as a freelance nutritionist and recommend food and diet programs to people who want to become fit and healthy. Of course, this is just an example. The possibilities are endless and would depend on your learned skill or any skill that you are willing to learn.

## Promote your freelance or online business

No matter how good you are, it will be a challenge to have clients or customers if the market is not even aware that you exist. You should understand that the online world is a big world out there. Although you have the potential to reach a big market, the level of competition is also tight. Other people offer the same services as you do. These people are also putting in time, money, and effort to promote their services. However, you do not have to directly compete with them. The important thing is for you to do something to make the market know that your business exists and that you are ready and able to offer them your services. So, how can you effectively spread the word about your services? Here are notable things that you should do:

- Call to action

Make sure that your blog posts make use of a call to action. What is a call to action? As the name implies, it is about telling your readers what to do. This is usually added at the end of an article. For example, you can write something like this: *If you are looking for a _____, then click here.* You can then lead your readers to a page where you offer your products or services. This way, you first give your audience some useful information which helps build trust. After that, you get to offer them your services. As you can see, it is important that you provide your readers with helpful contents; otherwise, they will probably not consider hiring your services or buying your products, as the case may be.

A call to action has to be short yet direct. Limit it to just one or two short sentences. The important thing is to direct the readers to what you want them to read next. Do not make it seem as if you were trying to deceive your readers. Instead, you should make it look natural as if you are just helping or guiding your readers. This is not a form of manipulation but should be more like offering help to the readers through your services.

- Improve your SEO

By writing contents optimized for SEO, you can increase your site's/blog's visibility online. Take note that every new visitor that you lead to your site is a potential customer. The more that you improve your SEO ranking, the more people will find your site. Hence, make sure to observe the best SEO practices with every post that you make.

- Share on social media

Of course, when it comes to making a noise and informing people about something, social media tops the list. This is why you need to work on having a strong and quality following on social media. Now, the problem is when you have just started to use social media or you simply do not have any good following. In this case, you can start building a strong network of connections now. A good way to do this quickly is to look for someone who is active and already has a strong following on the niche or subject related to your business. Try to establish a good connection with this person by writing comments or sharing his works. If you do this to several people, chances are that some of them would also share your work, and this is a good way to tap a big market and gain more followers. Of course, to increase the chances of success, you need to make sure that you provide high-quality contents.

Now, when you share or promote your business on social media, you need to observe some ethical rules. You should not bombard your connections with lots of posts. As a rule, only promote your own stuff around 3-5 times a day. You should also learn to support and promote others. Take note that when you use social media, you should also learn to focus on other people. If you want others to give you any attention, then you should also give them attention.

You should also not post a full article. Instead, just write a good short introduction to hook a reader, and then provide a link to your blog or website. You should also include a picture. According to research, you can get more clicks if also include a picture to your posting. Needless to say, the image should be relevant to your article.

- Support group

There is nothing wrong with asking for some support from your family and friends. This can be very helpful, especially when you are just starting out. If you have a friend who is active and has a good following on social media, then that is a big plus. You do not have to beg people to help promote your site. If you are not comfortable asking for help, then simply let them know that you have a website or blog. Out of goodwill, it is up to them if they would like to help you promote it. This is an effective way to get followers quickly.

- AdWords

Perhaps one of the best ways to promote your online or freelance business especially when you are just starting out is to use AdWords. AdWords is a Google program that will allow you to promote your site or blog by displaying Google ads on search engines and other pages. This is a paid service, but it is very much worth it. Unlike other ad programs, you will only be charged when somebody actually clicks on your advertisement. If your ads are only viewed and not clicked, then you do not have to pay anything. Hence, you truly get your money's worth. You only pay when a person actually sees your page. You also have the option to choose any part of your blog or site where you will lead your audience. If you are just starting out and still have some issues with gaining visibility online and withdrawing traffic to your blog, then Google AdWords can be very helpful. And, since it is owned by the Internet giant, Google, you know that you can rely on it.

Another interesting feature of using AdSense is that you can use targeted keywords. This means that your ads will only appear when certain keywords are searched for in the search box. You can also target the countries and even specific cities where you want your ads to appear. Thus, if you just want your ads to appear in the US or any particular city or cities therein, then you can do that as well. The cost is also very much reasonable. You can adjust and specify just how much you are willing to spend per click.

When you use AdWords, you will also be the one who will design the advertisement that will appear. The key is to make your advertisement short, direct, and catchy. Also, make sure that you have a good page where you direct your audience after they click on your ad. If you are selling a product, say, an ebook, then you can direct them to your sales page.

- Specialized page/ Sales page

This is probably the most important part of a blog room website. This is where you feature your product or service and convince people to hire or buy from you. Here, you will highlight your product/service and make your offer. Of course, you do not have to make it obvious that you want to make a sale or be hired. Rather, a person who visits this page should feel and know that he needs to hire you. Or, in case you are selling something, that he would want to buy it. Instead of telling people to buy your product, you should let them know why they would want to buy what you offer. This page should identify a problem and a solution to that problem. Of course, the solution to that problem would be whatever it is that you offer.

You might also want to read on copywriting or even hire a professional copywriter to write your sales page.

# Step 5 — Quit Your Job

Okay, so here is the last step. Unlike the previous one, you should now be sure that you can support yourself and your family even if you let go of your present job. By this time, you should already have your 6 months of savings, as well as a profitable side income, which could be your online or freelance business. Since you have enough savings for 6 months, the side income does not need to generate such money to cover for all of your bills. But, of course, you should make it as profitable as possible. After all, this is the part where you will embark upon a new path in your life. It is also worth noting that this is not saying goodbye to work. Rather, this is more about living the life that you want, which includes having the work that you have always wanted. Hence, you will still make money in the process. However, you simply cannot expect the transition to happen quickly, so it is best to have some money in reserve.

Okay, so this step is more concerned about quitting your job. This is where you ask yourself if you can now safely quit your job. How much savings do you have? Will you be able to support yourself for 6 months without any problem? Are you sure that you want to leave your secured 9-5 job?

Once you reach this step, it is not unusual to suddenly feel confused or uncertain; however, this is a decision that you need to make. You need to be objective about this. You should honestly assess the situation. There are two opposing forces that you should be careful with. The first one is fear. Fear is where you can now quit your job and live the life that you have always wanted, but since you are full of fear, you deprive yourself from having this chance. This is where you cling to your secured 9-5 job even though you know that it does not give you fulfillment or happiness. Fear can prevent you from taking the next step and making positive changes. Remember that in life you need to take risks. This is how you can grow and develop. If you do not take risks, then you will always be stuck in the routine that you want to escape from.

The next hindrance to your success would be the opposite of fear, and that is being too arrogant to the point that you fail to recognize your weaknesses. The problem here is that you do not make the necessary changes or adjustments. So, if you realize that what you have is not enough to support you and your family from 6 months and that your side income is also not enough to provide your needs, then do not quit your job right away. Do not make big assumptions that you will soon be successful. You have to consider your obligations and be sure that you will be able to meet all of your obligations.

Instead of submitting to fear or arrogance, you should be more careful by taking the right approach and being more confident. Confidence comes from knowledge and being assured of your capabilities. When assessing your situation, you should be honest and face all of the facts of the situation.

It is noteworthy that finally quitting your job is a very serious decision that will surely have an impact on your life, so this is definitely something that you have to consider seriously. You should realize that if you do not quit your job, then you will forever be trapped in your current routine. This means that you might never be able to live the life that you have always wanted.

**Take the step – only once you have 6 months savings and if you have a side income that replaces your main income**

Once you are sure that you are ready, when you know that you have enough savings for 6 months and that you also have a profitable side income that you can rely on, then it is time for you to take the step.

This is it! This is what you have worked for all this time. This is the moment when you finally leave your job and jump into the life that you have always dreamed of.

Whatever you want to do, then now is the time to do it. However, you should not forget about your responsibilities. Also, keep in mind that you still have to manage your online or freelance business even just as a side income as you work on whatever it is that you want to do.

If what you what to do is the online or freelance business that you have, then now is the time to go all in and work on it full time.

Taking this step is a very serious matter, but this is also what you have prepared for all this time. Finally, you can now live the life that you have always wanted. You are now in the position where you can take risks since you have enough buffer zone or margin for error. Of course, it was not easy to reach this stage, so make the most out of what you have. If your side income or business also happens to be your dream work, then you are in the perfect position. Still, either way, it is now just a matter of doing your best and experiencing the life that you have always wanted.

Now, many people, when they reach this point, they become afraid. This is true, especially when you are already used and have grown dependent on your 9-5 job, and this is understandable. After all, your current setup has already allowed you to gain 6 months of savings, which means that you are already doing well, so why take a sudden change? Another problem here is that it might be difficult for you to go back to your job after you quit. When thinking about the situation this way, the most logical reason would be for you to just remain as you are. However, you need to understand that doing so will not get you anywhere. If you limit yourself now and do not take risks, then you will never have the chance to live the life that you have always wanted. You have to understand that for you to live your dream life, then you need to take risks and sacrifices. As the saying goes, you cannot discover a new island without losing sight of the shore.

If you are afraid that you might not be able to return to your current work after you quit, you might want to take the time to talk with your boss about it. There is a good chance that he will be able to understand your situation. In fact, he might even encourage you to pursue your dream and give you some pieces of advice. Since you have reached this point, the recommended thing to do would be to pursue what you have always wanted.

So, this is it. Finally you can transition to the life that you want. You deserve it. You do not have to look back, but you have all the reasons and inspiration to look forward. With 6 months of savings and a profitable side income, you can now afford to take risks without any worry. This is why the preparation was also quite intense. After all, building six months of savings is not a joke. This is because, by the time you reach this point, you can finally put all your focus on whatever it is that you have always wanted without any worry. Make sure to do your best.

You might want to give yourself about two or three days to take a relaxing break before you fully transition to the kind of life that you want. If you do, use that time to relax and prepare yourself for a new journey that is to come. This is the best time for you to make your own reflections. Learn from your past and have a positive attitude towards the journey that is ahead of you. It is worth noting that this is not the end of your journey or work. In fact, this is only the beginning of a life that you have always dreamed of. Now, it is time for you to live that life and be successful. Do not think that there will be no challenges. No matter what path you take, especially if it is a meaningful one, then you should always expect challenges. These challenges will reveal your strengths and weaknesses, and they will make you grow as a person. Do not run away from challenges. Instead, face them with courage. Keep in mind that every mountain has its own risks and obstacles. If it is too easy to climb, then perhaps it is not worth climbing.

For now, this is your moment. You should make the best out of it. Finally, it is time for you to live the life that you have always wanted. Do not be afraid. Believe in yourself and make it count.

# Best Practices

To increase your chances of success, you also need to learn certain best practices. These practices will ensure that you are able to execute the lessons in this book effectively. Let us discuss them one by one:

- Research

If you have a blog or site where you provide your audience with quality information, then be sure to do thorough research. Make sure that you give them facts and reliable information. This is how you build trust. As you already know by now, building trust is a very important element of your success. You do this by providing your readers with helpful information. To ensure that you give them the kind of information that your readers need, you have to do research. Now, many people do their research but fail to do sufficient research. There are no hard and fast rules as to what constitutes sufficient research. However, you can tell if the amount of research you have made is enough when you are confident and could justify everything that you have written. Needless to say, you should also cite your sources to avoid plagiarism issues. As much as possible, only cite from reputable sources. Even when you are engaged in the businesses of selling other people's products or affiliate marketing, it is your job to provide your audience with honest and useful information. Again, doing thorough research is the key to doing this. Make sure that every post that you make is backed up by a solid research. Never make assumptions, unless you make it clear to your readers that you are just making a reasonable assumption. Do your research at all times to provide high-quality information.

- Do not overthink

A common mistake is to keep on thinking when you are already in the process of execution. Of course, this does not mean that you should no longer think and reconsider what you are doing; however, you should avoid overthinking. A good way to do this is to have a plan. A plan should be made prior to execution. Once you start working on a plan, then make sure that you spend most of your time taking positive actions instead of overthinking. You are free to give yourself some time each day to think and reconsider your decision, but be sure to limit the time that you spend doing it. You do not want your focus to be divided. This is another reason why you should not rush with coming up with a plan. Once you have a plan, then know that it is time for you to execute it. You can still change your original plan if you realize that it is for the best after a careful consideration of the circumstances.

- Use links (inbound and outbound links)

Learn to incorporate links in your articles. A link acts as a call to action that directs a reader what to do next. An easy and effective way of doing this is by using a hyperlink. You can add a hyperlink to a particular phrase in your article that will lead the reader to another page, which could be a page in your blog or outside of your blog. If you direct your readers to another page within your blog, then that is referred to as an inbound link. If you refer your reader to a page outside of your blog, then that is referred to as an outbound link. You can use an outbound link whenever you cite a source. You can use an inbound link to direct your reader to another relevant article in your blog. This is a good way to make your articles promote themselves. However, avoid using too many links in an article. As a general rule, you can limit the use of links to just around 2 or 3 per article, depending on its length. Of course, the longer an article is, the more links you can use. Just avoid making it look like being bombarded with links.

- Offer a freebie

People love free stuff. The good thing is that when a person likes something that they got from you from freelance, the more they will be interested in your work. A good way to do this is to give them a free ebook on your site. This is how so many bloggers draw more followers. But, of course, before you can expect for anyone to think about downloading your ebook, you should make sure that your blog or site is already filled with useful information. The articles on your site are also something that you offer for free. The more that people like your blog posts, the more likely that they will want to download your free ebook.

- Grow your email list

It does not matter what kind of business or service that you offer. It is always important to focus on growing your email list. What is an email list? It is a list of subscribers to your blog or website. You are probably familiar with the *subscriber's* button that appears on most blogs. When a person subscribes to your blog, you can send him an email at any time. Subscribers will also be notified every time you make a new post on your blog. A good way to make people subscribe to your mailing list is by offering them a free ebook in exchange. After all, they are free to unsubscribe at any time.

- Respond to comments

If you manage a blog, be sure to respond to comments. This is a good way to establish a connection with your followers or readers. It does not matter whether you received one or even a hundred comments. As much as possible, you should respond to every comment. This is common ethics in the online world. You have to appreciate that the person has taken the time to write a comment, so it is only right and just that you give an appropriate response. This is a good way to build a good relationship with a reader. Take as much time as you need. The important thing is to make every person know that you are giving him attention. A simple "Thank you." would be enough, if you cannot say anything else.

Now, there are primarily two kinds of comments that you will receive: positive and negative. Of course, there is no problem when you receive a positive comment. However, how should you deal with a negative comment? You have to understand that negative comments are not completely bad. Although a negative comment might make you feel insulted, you should learn to relax when you read a negative comment. Try to find out if the said negative comment has any basis or not. You should realize that every negative comment is an opportunity to make improvements. However, there are also negative comments that are completely unreasonable. As a rule, this is how you should deal with a negative comment: If it is reasonable, then thank the one who commented as he/she helped you to improve. That is something that you should appreciate. However, if the negative comment was made simply to say something bad, you can either just ignore it or give a polite reply like a simple "Thank you." without having to explain anything else. After all, your other readers and followers will know if a certain comment is true or not.

If a person who commented on your work also has a blog, it is advised that you also visit his blog and comment on his posts. This is a good way to establish new connections and build a good relationship. After all, in the online world, bloggers usually help and support one another.

- Join related groups and forums

It is strongly advised that you join related online groups and forums. No matter what your business is, you will surely find related groups online. By joining these groups, you can connect with people who can be your potential clients or customers, as well as meet people who might be able to help you with your business. It is also free to join such groups online, and it usually takes just a few clicks of the mouse. Social media channels always have groups that you can join. With regard to forums, there are many forums online that. You can participate in it. Sometimes it also helps to just read the posts, and you will surely find some interesting posts from time to time.

- Be patient

Establishing your presence online or even just on social media will definitely take time. Even if you follow all the best blogging practices in the world, it will take some time before you can establish a strong following. Therefore, you have to be patient. Be patient and persevere. Do not worry; once you are able to establish your business online, it will be easier to get more work or projects.

- Connect with the right people

Connect with the right people. The quality of your connections can determine the extent of your reach in the market. The right people are those who have a strong following. Although quantity may also matter, it is more important to focus on the quality of your connections.

This does not mean that you should ignore other people. Rather, it just tells you where you should focus on.

Especially when you are just starting out, do not expect for these people to just connect with you. It is your job to take steps to find and connect with them. If you notice someone who has a good and strong following, then try to establish a connection with him. As we have already discussed, you can easily do this by writing a comment on his posts. Now, the key here is to write a grabbing comment that will make him/her take notice of you. If you get lucky, he might also comment and share your work with his network, and this is a great way to tap a wide network of new connections. Now, do this several times, and you will surely end up with a good following as long as you also do your part and provide quality information and/or service.

- Quality is your main priority

No matter what kind of business or online job you do, take note that quality remains to be the most important thing. In fact, even an article without any SEO techniques can gain lots of traffic provided it has a good quality, such as being able to provide helpful information and details. Now, whether you work as a freelancer or programmer or anything else, the way to have continuous business/projects is to render quality work. Otherwise, it will be hard for your client to refer you to another or to rehire your services.

A common mistake is to try to quickly set up your freelance career or online business. This has a tendency to end up with lots of low-quality stuff. You need to take your time, especially when you are just building your foundation. Do not rush the process.

- "You are the average of the five people around you."

This may not be directly related to the job that you have, but it has an effect on your performance. What this saying means is that you should be careful with the people with whom you associate with. Hence, it is advised that you associate with those who will make you feel more motivated and inspired. Surround yourself with positive and successful people, or at least with those who inspire you to be a better person. These are the people who have a strong influence in your life.

- Time management

Time is money. When you go to work, mostly, you will also be paid per hour. If you know the value of your time, then you would surely what to manage how you spend it. You should have a schedule that is conducive to your work. But, do not end up with a schedule that is full of nothing but work, remember that you also need to rest and take a break from time to time. You should manage your time properly, especially when you have a family. Take note that you also need to spend time with your spouse and kids, if any. After all, what good is all the work that you do if you just live only for yourself?

- Learn from your competitors

You should learn from your competitors. No matter what online business or freelance service that you offer, you will surely have some competitors. Business competition is part of the market. If there is no competition, then perhaps you are in the wrong market. Instead of feeling bad that other people offer a similar service or product as you do, you should learn from them. Do this by comparing your strengths and weaknesses. Again, the strengths and weaknesses of your business are relative to the strengths and weaknesses of your competitors. You should try to further improve your strengths. You should also work on your weaknesses; otherwise, you might get left behind the competition. Competition is not really a bad thing, depending on how you view it. If you use it to improve yourself and your business, then you can say that it is good and healthy.

- Take a break

It is good to be hardworking. In fact, you are encouraged to work hard and to always do your best. However, you need to understand that it will take time before you can achieve your objective and to be able to establish your freelance or online business. You also need to take a break. If you allow some time to clear your mind and give yourself a break, then you will be more effective. Now, a common mistake is to take a rest but then continue to think about your problems while on a break. This will only make you feel more stressed. When you take a break, use that time wisely to really take a break and relax. This is the best time for you to go on a vacation or even spend just a movie night at home with your family. The important thing is to relax and have fun. Do not worry; after the break, you are expected to work even harder.

# Conclusion

Thanks for making it through to the end of this book. I hope it was informative and able to provide you with all of the tools you need to achieve your goals whatever they may be.

The next step is to apply everything that you have learned. It is time for you to take positive actions and make positive changes in your life.

This book is actually a journey of change. Indeed, by the time you take the last step, you have already made lots of wonderful changes. It should be noted that change is within your power to do, but it requires that you take actions to make them happen.

As you follow the lessons in this book, you will be faced with challenges and hardships, and this is also how you will see and appreciate your own strengths. Of course, it will also let you know about your weaknesses. Now, this is important. Some people shy away from knowing their weaknesses, and so they fail to do something about them. The more weaknesses that you are able to identify the more chances you have at improving yourself and your business. Indeed, this journey is not just about making more money, but it can also change your life for the best.

If you want to make changes in your life, then you need to take positive actions. You cannot just wait and expect for something to happen out of nowhere. You need to realize that you have the power to make things happen. You do not have to rely on anything else but yourself. You simply have to do your best, especially when you know that there are people who also depend on you for support. Still, even though you may have a family that relies on you, it does not mean that you should no longer strive to live the life that you have always wanted. After all, your family also wants you to be happy, and they want you to be successful. If you truly succeed in your chosen path whatever that may be, you will surely be in a far better position than you are right now. There is nothing that compares to a life where you are happy and satisfied with what you do and have. The thing is that you can have that life that you have always wanted. You simply have to give yourself a chance to achieve it. This book is your ticket that shows you the way to your dreams. However, knowledge alone is not enough. You have to put that knowledge into practice to take your dream into reality. Since this is a journey to achieve your dream life, it is only right that you give it your best.

Finally, if you found this book useful in anyway, a review on Amazon is always appreciated!

www.ingramcontent.com/pod-product-compliance
Lightning Source LLC
Chambersburg PA
CBHW071225220526
45468CB00002B/733

\* 9 7 8 1 7 2 2 3 5 0 9 1 8 \*